Gwendolyn
MacEwen

THE
FIRE-EATERS

An Oberon Book

For everyone who has passed through fire and survived

Early Middle Age

is a stage before the Renaissance
when all the glamorous crimes of youth
return to bug and prod you into being

and all your friends blame everything
on comets and petroleum

and meanwhile all the birds are singing
so loud and shrill
the sulphur colour of their song
is miles beyond your knowing

you find that you are not complaining
when cities disappear in the middle of the night
and axioms are no longer right

the sky is an oil-slick
the fish are slowly figuring out the sea

a hairless wonder will be born again
man will be born again
you will be born again
scared silly or suddenly sane

and you'd be ready if you knew when

January

I wouldn't want to speak the truth
But you know what I mean
The woman said
Who had no teeth

I do not mean what I have said
Said the man who was planning
On losing a leg

I have come to terms at last with winter
I have a gentleman's agreement with my pain
But I am not a gentleman

The fact that I am 34
The year perhaps of many unborn
Sisters / brothers
Should not bother me or you

I say again
I have a gentleman's agreement with my pain

Brother, lead me up the evil stairs
That lead to God

Lead me up the goddam frozen
Broken stairs that lead to God

Lead me by the head or hand
Lead me by the hand or head
All up the slimy shiny stairs
To God

I have a gentleman's agreement with my pain

What Is Tooth?

What is tooth? the dentist said, as he
Washed his hands in the porcelain bowl

It's something that grows in my head (I said)
Like a mean white cancer or a wall

You mean it's something like a brainstorm
Or a maelstrom, then, or a sign of
Wisdom or a pall?

Your gums are receding far too fast, said he.
So is the sea, I said.

A thing or fang is growing
Into the upper right side of my skull
Where my soul consorts with tigers
And many crimes commit themselves

I do not understand you, not at all
Wise lady, for I see the tooth of wisdom,
Truth-stone stuck inside your gum

My tongue would try to free it
But I speak a foreign tongue

This tooth, would you believe, at my age
Tries cutting through my will
A will that flirts with eagles
And besides, my jaw's too small

I think I see a sandstorm or a snowstorm
In the mind, the dentist said
As he stepped slowly through the wall

I won't get wise, I tell you!
And this small white stone will not get born.
I have friends whose jaws shoot straight up into heaven
I have other foolish teeth which drop out and resign

Not in this small mouth will Wisdom grow. God no.

Your gums are receding far too fast, said he.

So is the sea, I said, just so.

Teeth

I can outlive every war
I can relive every war
In my guts or in
My toothroots which protest
Mortality

Last night my dentist died

There was blood on my pillow
And some will say I lied
When I woke up then and shouted
"Someone died!"

Last night my dentist died

The cavities in my molars and my soul
Will get stuffed with porcelain and poetry
And God will be defied
With a brand-new white morality

Last night my dentist died

Molars and mortality, I said
The roots of the great world-tree are denied
And I play with words and stuff them
Under the pillow of my head and pray
A dime or quarter will appear
In their place on the following day

I can outlive every war
And still be less alive
Than the corpses in Leningrad
Than the simplest burnt-out star

And I'm tired of having a sixth sense
And would rather have six cents from
The solar tooth, stone of my head
Which some magician may extract
And bury beneath my bed

I sleep, and many will deny
That truth hurts more than teeth
And anyway

Last night my dentist died

Hands

There was one of those ads in the Toronto Star *about the kid you adopt for today.* Today's Child, *or something like that. There was nothing much wrong with him except that he was Indian/Black/Blue/Smiles a Great Deal and Has Hands that Unfortunately are Constantly Turned Upward.*

When my husband speared the octopus
And brought it to the stone

The tentacles turned on to life
And wrapped themselves around his arm

He said, *Now look, it will not die
Unless you dash it much upon the stone*

Which I did, but God, it hung on
So damn tight I nearly broke my arm

I smashed it till its suds came out like Tide
A soapy mush in the lagoon

Its pinky colour disappeared
Upon the salty stone

Yer average octopus is used to this:
(the sea-spear and the salty stone)

Its brains are splocked against a rock
And it does not blame anyone

Its only sin was its tastely ugliness
Whether its arm-legs were eight or seven

And I have forced a rhyme because
Today's Child's only sin was that

His palms turned upward, always
Into heaven

The Allergist

The nurse made twenty scratch-tests on my arm
The allergist made twenty needle-things
On my other
Arm

I waited twenty minutes, or
Was it 40
For the terrible verdict
Concerning my specific
Allergies

And then I learned the ghastly truth
Concerning ragweed, early-summer earth,
Cats and poplar trees
And would you believe, the Maple Leaf?

I cannot be allergic to the Maple Leaf
I said
As I slowly arose from the metal bed

But it shows right here, my dear,
The allergist said
Expertly checking my upper arm
And peering professionally into my head

I cannot be allergic to the Maple Leaf
I said
As I slowly arose from the metal bed

But you are, my dear
And it shows right here
But it can be cured, he said

What else am I allergic to, I said
Oh, nothing much except your cats and house-dust
And your new spring grass and your old ragweed.
You mean I should avoid the world and go to seed?
Oh no, it can all be cured, he said.

Kohoutek

Before the comet came
All my friends were going sane
And it was terrible to see

All my friends said: Things will die and rise
I closed my eyes

Before Xmas it was there, I swear,
Across the street above a broken tree
And it was terrible to see
It broke my eyes

I cut my hair
I cried

Then I got sick with fire in my gut
For three weird weeks, and on the bed
There were these luminous animals
Which slept with me, and which
Came singing from my head

It was and was not there, you see.
Kohoutek sang above the broken tree

It did no good, it did no harm
The wars went on as always
And the comet was a quiet bleeding storm

But could it be that

Out of such bright evils
Out of suchlike brilliant ills
We rise and die and finally get born?

A Seminar at York,
August 1973

Funny how all things revolve in the Druidic circle
of these trees

Some things revolve in air and have the gall to call
themselves birds

Some things resolve to be stones, but I know differently

I spend so long among your people, God, that I
forget that once the wicked wheels of God start
turning
they don't stop

Any more than birds stop birding
or the world stops being
wild murder of the first order
and sole residence of a worried Lord

(In-breeder of angels and the only God)
Funny how all things revolve in the Druidic circle
of these trees

Fragments from a Childhood

You are eleven years old and have finally decided you can fly. You've been through all the issues of the Marvel Family comics for the last three years, and you know the key word that will give you wings. You can fly if you pretend your white satin bed-jacket is a cape.

Now for you Shazam of the Creative Word, the Logos, the formula of flight. You know you can fly, the way They do, straight out like a bullet with your arms stretched forward and your cape fluttering in the wind.

There is no doubt in your mind.

Something else delays you.

You've tied the white satin bed-jacket around your neck tightly so that the wild sleepy folds fall down properly from the shoulders. You imagine what the wind will do to it; you know what it means.

You have many words to utter before you reach Shazam. You speak them slowly, half-hoping you will not reach the end of them, half-hoping that the world will not wring from you the Final Formula, for everything would stop then. You don't really want to pronounce the Unpronounceable.

You stand poised over the steep ravine that leads down to the river. You know it will work because it works for the Marvel Family. You think about the other kids who read the same comics but who don't know what they are all about. They *don't* know, otherwise they'd be here with you above the ravine with their bed-jackets tied around their necks, wouldn't they, wouldn't they? Maybe they do it alone in their rooms, maybe they pose alone in front of their mirrors, but none of them are here where you are now.

In a way you really do want to have the Great Word wrung out of you, but until now you've witheld it, having sworn never to pronounce it except in a moment of extremity. After all, you don't wish to destroy the world. . . .

It's a long way down to the bottom of the ravine. There are no witnesses. You wanted it that way, didn't you?

Maybe God will punish you for your insolence. Icarus tried it once; Prometheus still lies chained to a rock with an eagle picking at his liver for a crime less than this. But the Marvel Family has no quarrel with God, and besides they do Good Works and have a fine sense of humour; God never punished them because they were Super.

Neither does Wonder Woman; she's a pagan and swears by obscure Greek deities. Anyway, you don't like her much because her costume is so American; Mary Marvel's costume is a hundred times better, although in the last issue her skirt was lengthened to below the knees and you were so mad you were going to write in to the editor about it.

You're still murmuring the introductory words; you realize you're coming to the end and in a minute you're going to have to say Shazam and take off into thin air above the ravine.

You know you can do it.

Something else delays you.

Well, the Marvel Family is so trite, for one thing. They just fly around, they never *discuss* anything. Are they aware of INFINITY for instance? Are they?

Do they know the Word is Ineffable, for instance?

Can any one of them even *spell* Ineffable?

You are trembling now and you say to yourself: Now I begin to suspect that my soul is greater than the soul of Mary Marvel. I've always known, deep down, that the Marvel Family are not very intelligent even though they fly and lightning shoots down and claims them.

Are they really interested in their marvels? Or do they just fly around, poor fools, casually tossing off the Word?

Can they even SPELL the Word?

Holey Moley, all they can do is DO IT, for heaven's sake! But you, you can THINK about it, you know what it MEANS!

Suddenly you pity their lemon-yellow lightning bolts and their plastic boots. If Mary Marvel's skirt hadn't been lengthened, you might never have come to this moment of truth. You walk away in your white satin bed-jacket, sadder but wiser. It starts to rain and your miraculous cape drips all down your back.

Something has come to pass, you think, something more important than a mere flight over the ravine.

More Fragments

It's about a year later and the gang from the other neighbourhood has declared war on your gang. The challenge has been accepted, and you are about to lead your army into battle. It is Sunday and the streets are empty. You are calm and deliberate; you brandish yourself with one large stick. You march quietly with your men through the six blocks between you and the enemy.

Now you see them approaching; their leader also carries a big stick. The armies halt; there is a moment or two of total silence.

You think: There are no limits to the world.

By unspoken agreement, you and the enemy leader leave your gangs and approach each other in the Sunday street. Neither of you has any argument with the other, but a principle is a principle. Some great wrong has been committed that has led to this war; it does not matter that no-one can remember what it was.

You face each other now, not two yards apart. You stare. The battle always begins with Eyes.

He says: You wanna prove something?

You say: Yes, I wanna prove something.

He says: Think you can prove it?

You say: Yeah, I can prove it.

He says: What do you wanna prove?

You say: What do *you* wanna prove?

You stare some more.

He says: You really think you can prove it, eh?

You say: Yeah, I can prove it.

He says: Okay, you wanna prove it now?

You say: Listen, I'll prove it anytime.

You stare some more. Tired of the conversation, you

suddenly lift your stick high as a warning.

He says: So! Trying to prove something, eh?

You stand there with your stick held high, your face glowing.

He says: Wanna prove it next week after school?

You say: Sure, anytime.

You both turn away and walk back to your men. The gang asks you: Hey, what happened anyway?

You allow a moment or two to pass before answering. Then you casually fling your stick away and say: I told him we could prove it, anytime.

Your men nod their heads in profound acceptance, and you all walk back the six blocks to your home base. It is Sunday, about noon. No-one will ever know what went on out there when the two generals met in the bright white Sunday streets.

Last Fragments

Today there's nothing much going on, so you and your friend Jonathan decide to crawl into the back trunk of a little Austin in a parking lot, to prove that you can both fit. You cram yourselves into the trunk and close the door. You lie there in silence, starting to get bored all over again when Jonathan says

—Hey, I think the door got locked by accident.

—What do you mean? you ask.—You didn't pull it down tight, did you?

—Yeah, I think I did.

—Jerk. So that means we're locked in, right?

—Looks like it.

—I guess these things can't be opened from the inside, right?

—I guess not.

You and Jonathan lie there in the cramped darkness; at first you're sort of glad that there's something to do, that the day won't be a total loss. Then you start to wonder.

—So I guess we're actually locked in, sort of?

—Yeah. Hey, do you think people can suffocate in places like this?

—Who ever heard of suffocating in the back trunk of an *Austin*, jerk?

—Well, who cares what kind of a car it is? It's a trunk, that's all.

—There's no-one around the parking lot, eh?

—No.

—So how long do you think the air will last? Do you suppose we should call out?

—Okay, let's call out a few times, but remember to conserve the AIR. Call out, but breathe as little as possible, got it?

—How am I supposed to call out if I'm not supposed to BREATHE, for heaven's sake? By calling out we're using up AIR, aren't we?

—I didn't mean it like that.

—If we call out we'll use up the air SOONER!

—Look, we gotta do SOMETHING!

—Holy God, will you stop shouting and using up all the AIR!

—Who's shouting, you're the one who's SHOUTING!

—I'm using up less air than YOU, that's for sure!

—That's not true! I'm hardly breathing PERIOD!

—We should shut up because we're using AIR, and we need the air to SHOUT!

—You're the one who's using it UP!

—If you don't SHUT UP we'll SUFFOCATE!

—Okay, let's whisper. Try not to breathe at all.

Jonathan produces a safety pin from his jeans and begins to poke little holes in the inner lining of the trunk.

—What good's that going to do?

—It'll make more air, that's what, pinholes. . . .

He pokes some more.

—Jonathan, do you know how much air the average human being consumes in an average minute? you ask him in a ghastly whisper.

—Never mind how much, I'm poking for more. You gotta make use of whatever you got on hand. I plan to poke till I've got a hole big enough to get my hand through.

—With a safety pin? Holy God, you'll be poking for centuries!

—Well, it's little things like this that save people's lives, and I gotta do SOMETHING!

Don't SHOUT, you're stealing the AIR again!

—I told you not to BREATHE, stupid! If you breathe

25

you'll just use up the air that I'm getting through the pin-holes, and then we're NOWHERE, understand?

So I should stop BREATHING and DIE so you can lie there and poke!

—Well, if we used the air we had five minutes ago and shouted like I said, we could be saved by NOW!

—Hey Jonathan, can you breathe?

—I'm too tired to poke anymore, it's no use, it's all your fault. I needed more air than you because I was using the safety pin. Now. . . it's too late. . . .

H—E—L—L—P

Mineral Water

Caves of steel and caves of ice
My thoughts have all turned into stalactites

I will boil nickels all my life
And jewelry and rusty nails

And drink the brew to show my mettle
And to feel

As healthy as the man in the iron mask
Or a well-tempered clavier.

The best mineral water you can buy
Is bottled in Germany where they boil

Valkyries and their metal spears
In caves of steel and caves of ice

My thoughts have all turned into stalactites

What Am I Waiting For?

At first I didn't even know I *was* waiting for anything at all
except for nights to fall as they had to, and for suns to rise.

My brain, then, was a mountain lion, lofty and watchful,
assessing the terrain below with brute magnificent scorn

My heart made tracks like a cougar, and I walked in the
murderous whiteness of the universe without harm

I could get through each minute; each minute was most
certainly a hoop of fire my Trainer bade me leap through
with brute grace

Now walking home at night through streets baptized by
rain I feel It waiting for me as surely as I am awaiting It

And I walk faster for I am sure that this time It will be there
in my mailbox or tacked onto my door or stuck onto a wall

It will be addressed to me (who else?) and will bear the seal
of the Almighty and Most Perfect One, Lord of the Universe

Dear Gwen (It will call me by my familiar name), *Stop
waiting; All I have promised I have accomplished; the world
is whole again*

But it will not be there, I know it; It makes a point of not
being there ever never and forever, and that's bad

Because a promise I never knew was made to me, was broken
and a letter I never knew I waited for has failed to come

If one more sun rises without good reason I think I'll faint
and if I try to leap through one more minute in a hoop

Of life or fire
I will succumb

Horticulture

There are things one has to do
When the times are as ripe
As this unreal grass

I planted a bulb upside-down
By mistake
And imagined it would flower
In Hell, red as anything

After which I dug it up
And planted it right-side-up
And hoped that it would
Dig its way to Heaven

It goes without saying that these airplanes above me now
Are not flowers

It goes without saying that I have neither a green thumb
Nor a purple heart

It goes without saying that there are no flowers flying
In the sky

For the earth itself is dying

The Carnival

1

I danced before I learned to walk
And spoke before I learned to talk
I can do almost anything
But me myself I cannot sing.
Who am I, and who
Lives in the carnival behind my eye?

I swallow swords, I swallow fire
Twice a day for a very small fee
I am everyone's desire.
Do you know me?
I escape from ropes and chains
But I am not free, I am
The juggler juggling worlds behind your eye
I am the prisoner of me.

Who escapes from all the knots
The world can tie?
I swallow my words like swords
And cry
Who am I, and who
Lives in the carnival behind my eye?

2

I joined myself in the Mirror House
When all the children had gone home.
Hey! dancer, juggler, fire-eater, clown!
The crippled mirror stops you where you stand
The mirror has just stolen your left hand
And the whole glass house comes tumbling down.

I dance alone, I asked to dance alone
Inside the silver mirrors of my mind
Inside the living prison of my bones.

3

The wheel of the carnival turns forever
And I am its crazy seasonal rider.
I can't get off it, either
For when I paid my fare I said:
I want a ticket for the endless ferris
Let me on it, let me on!
And the man said: *It'll cost you plenty.*
And I answered:
I can't stand to see the great wheel empty,
Let me on it, let me on!
And he said: *Okay, man, it's your money.*

But it's funny because sometimes
I'm glad I can't get off it.
I circle, I rise, I fall.
I seem to move better than anyone below
Even though I can't move at all.

4

I danced before I learned to walk
And spoke before I learned to talk
I can do almost anything
But me myself I cannot sing.
Who am I, and who
Lives in the carnival behind my eye?

The singer who falls back into the song
The dancer who falls back into the dance
Houdini who falls back into his chains
To imprison himself again,
To laugh.
Who lives in the carnival which is you?
I do, I do.

5

Ladies and gentlemen I'll dance for you
Twice a day for a very small fee
Or I'll break chains and swallow fire
If you follow me.
I'll juggle worlds before your eyes
I am the way, I am the light.
Lock me up and I'll be free
To dance forever, if you follow me.

The Eagle

The Greeks have a dance called the zembekiko. *It is normally performed by a male dancer, who is either at the end or the beginning of his wits. Although one must adhere at all times to the strict and complex rhythm of the music, one is allowed all sorts of intricate variations, depending on one's ability and state of mind. The wisest time to attempt a* zembekiko *is when you are either totally sober or superbly drunk. Otherwise, the results may be disastrous, since you are likely to whirl like a dervish off the stage or swoon like a dying eagle in free fall. The dance is both a fight against gravity and a kind of flirtation with the earth. This should explain the following poem. Or perhaps the poem will explain the explanation, I'm not sure.*

Greeks have two ways of talking
—face to face or side to side—
One speaks and the other watches
The nearest wall
Where the birth of other worlds
Takes place before his eyes.

The imperial and impermanent eagle
Of the Byzantines
Had two heads that looked East and West
And tried to gather God
Into a single body
—the body of a bird—

I spoke before of a will that flirts
With eagles, and now I speak
Of eagles who flirt with earth
In their wide slow turning,
Their descent, their dialogue with death.

Then poised on some craggy cliff
Of mountain or of mind, they wait
For the updraft, breath of God, pure wind
To hoist them into heaven once again.

Whether with broken or unfailing wings
They fly, they rise, they fall

So with these dancers on the broken edge of midnight
Born with the sign of the double-headed eagle,
Dancing still.

Everyone Knows

That which we took so much for granted
—Holy poetry of water and of fire—
Is suddenly debatable.

Everyone knows where the universe ends
—Where the fire begins—
Insatiable.

What you watch with me now, my friend,
Is neither birth nor end
Nor anything tenable.

Sit with me, though, at this table!
Eat dreams and planets, all
Are edible.

Fire invites fire.

The One-legged Greek
with Gold Teeth

The man whose name is bigger than the universe
comes down from the mountain,
his smile shot with gold

Down from where the coils of ramhorns tell
tales you can't imagine, and
where names are multifold

Down from where a one-legged and imperfect God
breaks syllables cheap as stones
and the nights are cold

The man whose name is bigger than the universe
come down from the mountain with a bold mouth
and a bag of gold

To have his own teeth, speaking stones, withdrawn
and replaced with better ones
(of gold)

His name is Chrisostomos
who runs down from the mountain and declares:

Insofar as my shoe is a star
and my name is multifold, I dare
to make my mouth a fable full of gold

The streets are paved with syllables
and Chrisostomos sits in the dentist's chair

I cannot walk, my shoe is old
but Ah! My mouth is paved with gold

Animal Syllables

Let me say right off that this is no answer, for no question has as yet been posed. The gulls, merely, have gone mad out on the lake and have turned pure white for Christmas. Who has seen the future in retrospect? The lighthouse keeper at the end of the pier has nothing to say, and the great light rotates at the tip of the tower. The waves recur, the light, the seasons; memories flash and turn and guide the ships of wisdom in. I want to record the colours, the redness, the sea-green, the pure white; I want my syllables pure as the speech of gulls, or foxes.

The gulls are always screaming from the end of the long stone tongue which is the pier; the lake is always tasting the beach where once I lay beside the beachfire, my forehead facing Orion; the breakwater always chastises the waves, and the place where I pasted a poem with surf to a rock remains. It is earth, and surf, and blood; art is a small crime I commit against the seasons, or sometimes an elaborate lie my better sense rejoices in. And all the while the waves insist, present me with their patient, disciplined argument: *It has all been said before.*

The rocks talk, and the lighthouse describes Cabbalistic arcs all over the darkness. What colour was I wearing in September when the beach turned infra-red a second before the sunset? A red sweater, I remember now, and I bent over a strange shell. I could see the veins of my hands beneath the flesh; a black steamer passed silently through the channel; the shameless sun streamed over my left shoulder and set. Everything seemed gentle, and wild; a single gull was the Holy Spirit, a savage dove; a white dog was the violent Lamb. Dark, I built a beachfire and thought about the flames and the earth. In the darkness I constructed a fire; in the midst of the fire I began to gather another darkness.

The two cats, Cagliostro and Sundog, are constantly repairing themselves, combing, pulling, licking; it's almost as if they are able to anticipate some sort of ultimate wound and heal it in advance. The waves take care of the rocks in the same way, although they wear away with so much attention. Do all the soothing tongues of mothers, and seas, and lovers melt and wear away the flesh and rock they seek to heal? Do we die thin from the thousand kisses that drive the hurt away?

Kazmatla, I whisper (it is a word I have made up), *Kazmatla. I believe. Life is red, it is many colours.* Beyond these words is a private dance. It is as silent as that.

I went one midnight to the geometric gardens. Lakelight, the moon on lake, brought out the depths of their colours, and I stood close to where some dark water trickled through concrete slots. I could see only the red midnight flowers and the black basins of the fountains behind them. The flowers smelled stronger from a distance than they did right under the nostrils. Cinnamon and honey, acid.

I bent down over the water slots and shouted something, and the syllables were liquid syllables; they flowed down and away, out of the garden, toward the lake. They became the lake. I felt myself proceeding with ease from one reality to another, imagined myself creating and destroying each world of sensation I encountered.

Some time later I boiled eggs and ate my thin volumes of verse like fragile lettuce sandwiches. Then I think I wrote again with raving sanity: "The lake claims my face, the work of the surf is my body; I must remember those orderly, censured gardens. . . ."

I have begun to repair the house, having put it off for ages, deciding which aspect of it was most in need of repair.

Of erections, how few are domed like St. Peter's? I ask myself (Melville), as I hammer nails into the tottering walls.

Are there too many realities? I ask, as several of the nails fall out.

Art is affirmation; to lift the pen is to say Yes! I cry, as the wall and I support each other.

Then I begin to bring the outside in, that the house might be a small, select museum of the world. In the summer I bring driftwood, shells, flowers. There is no key to this place and, in a sense, no door. There is free passage in and out. Already small weeds shoot up between the floor and the wall. . . .

I tack up wallpaper that looks like wood (the walls were wood in the first place until the previous tenants covered them with dainty indoor scenes). I consider embroidering excerpts from the Cabbala on the cushion covers, or crocheting the writings of Kazantzakis on the tea-cosy, but I have no patience for such things. It seems I have one foot in one world and the other foot in another; I think I need new shoes.

Melville, it is said, read books about whales using whale-skins as bookmarks. . . .

When the ice-sheets groan and split on the lake they fracture the landscape for miles around. Today I bless the authors of our borders and boundaries—Columbus who I sometimes imagine anchored in mid-sea with America moving out like a great ship to discover *him*. Vast shorelines, tongues of continents like land-waves chasing the seas. Shorelines of souls, the beaches of consciousness strewn with a thousand little shells. . . .

The warehouses in the harbour turn gold at sunset; strange ships might sail in now from exotic foreign lands carrying ostrich feathers, elephant tusks, spices, silver filigreed bracelets, quinquiemec. . . . The snow-capped coalpiles are a mountain range in Tibet. Sundog the cat enters the house with snow on his eyebrows. All is well with the world. Somewhere out on the breakwater a single gull is preparing for some ultimate flight. Everything begins, everything is a continuum, everything organizes its death. There are red midnights of flowers, there are white midnights of snow. There are no alternatives to pain, there are no alternatives to beauty. The lighthouse describes great cryptic arcs across the darkness. We fold in upon ourselves like the waves, we fold under, falling in and out of the world's vision. How many languages can we know? We approach the end of utterance.

Kazmatla, Kazmatla, the waves insist it has all been said before. Somehow they must convince me, somehow I must believe them. The body has its own speech to be heeded now. Move swiftly in these snows, and leave no track.

The Great Horned Owl

Some time ago in Toronto
There was this great horned owl who hung around
The Granite Club
And attacked people as they came out by night

I gather that he hung onto their hair
And they were petrified with fright

Perhaps he just wanted to take them up to heaven
Perhaps he just wanted to make a scene
Or take them for a ride, or be owlish or whatever

At anyrate I'm sitting here
On a normal night, trying to figure out
What connection there must be

Between the hunchback of Notre Dame
And the great horned owl

Between Quasimodo and the great beast in the tree

Well, they both inhabited high places
And had a tendency to see people as rather small

Quasimodo swung from the bell-ropes singing
And laughing his way into a human hell

While the great horned owl twooped from his night-tree
And fastened his claws in the human skull

If I see the connection I will die with laughter
I will tumble off the universe
At the very least I might make verse
With the fulsome laughter of the moment
Yes, at last!

And I think the connection has to be
That when Quasimodo sat with the stone gargoyle
And looked down into the granite square below
He said (with his arm around the beast)
Why can't I be made of stone like thee?

In a world I do not have to suffer
On a couch where kittens quiver
I demand to be merely mortal
I command my self to endure

They did not have to kill King's mother
They did not have to be so sure
That death invokes another kingdom
Where red blood runs more pure

Than the putrid waters of their hatred
Or the nights whose birth was sperm
Oh life invokes another kingdom
Where lions and kittens swarm

Lip-service

The mist hangs down
like a grey nightgown
and the city
is a living mass of slaves

Who gets to be
the sovereign of flames?
Who's elected
the president of night?

Lead me to
the strange white horses of the morning

Drive me away from
the concealed stallions of the night

Poem

The moon's a mean eye between my two antennae

A man called George has just gone sane
And the neighbours call him simple

Since he plays Frisbee with the kids
In the middle of the road

And the sun's a golden moon between his eyes

The Clouds, the Birds
and the Wind

The clouds, the birds and the wind have no answer
even though no question has been posed.

And I suppose the thin and famous limbs of horses
can carry us nowhere
though they have flown on coluds.

I tend to go on
as my own wings get finally sewn on.

(The waves take long walks at midnight, and I live
with the mighty birds and roses.)

I submit the theory that the wind has no clothes.

Not with the Howling

not with the howling of these wolves, these
hot hounds of the morning
will I accept the messages of doom

out of the now non-visible night the stars
keep crawling

I wake and cough up clouds

for some reason days break just
before the dawn, and life is less
than temporary

I know the birds' wings hurt them, but
in order to exist, I eat
the bright ephemeral fruits of morning

last night's chicken wings, and apples,
eggs of an unreal dawn; I mourn
and the night-dogs go on barking

Lines for 999 Queen Street

A world where fear is normal and one seldom dares to live

A world where love is hungry and love-food can't be found

A world where God is willing but the spirits are so weak

A world where some go crazy and cannot find relief

It's a madhouse in my city or anywhere in the world

Where the cafeteria is huge and the food is small

Where the soup is thin and the interns are large

Where there's a piano in the corner no-one dares to play

The Aquarium: for J. S.

Death, perhaps, is a thing, or a fish, or a God

Do you recall your dreams when you are waking?
Yes, you dreamed that you'd been sleeping

Said the fish of many colours
Said the dim prime ministers of morning

Someone told me the movements of fish
Are so swift they are amazing

It is not boring, then, to screech
It is not boring to survive

Ours is the vision in our eyes
Ours is the message in the skies

I dreamt I woke up and fell
Head over heels into the water
Flat on my face into paradise

I've Been Painted

I've been painted with the colours of the morning

I would not be here but for a crescent moon

I would not be here but for the circle of the sun

Lord, could I take the poorest children in the world
And buy them all and make them happy?

Where were you when they needed you,
Landlord of the mountains?

I've been painted silver
I've been painted gold

All the trees are sold, and
My own flesh does not defend me

When the children die I'll buy
All the trees and mountains back

And they'll deceive me

God

You can't get above God, you know
My gardener said

I figured there was something wrong
Inside his head

And then there was an early dawn
Which tackled night and won

It came before the sun

God'll get back
My gardener said

I figured there was something wrong
inside his head

Fire

It's okay, I said, as I passed my hands over perfect fire.
It hurts, but this candle is not me, not you.

It's orange, red, green and blue.
It hurts, but it's not me, not you. It's fire.

Maybe I wounded the fire. I don't know.
It was itself, not me. See, I said, the snow

Can melt the fire (as I threw the candle out the window),
Flames burn bright as white, and all these colours

Are not worth our bleeding.

Second-degree Burns

My friend at the party said:
You'll get second-degree burns
If you keep sneaking through the fire

I wasn't sneaking
I was hovering with my hand
And anyway
It wasn't fire
But a candle

A candle involves fire, but
So does a hand

Trees involve fire
Streetcars involve fire

We all have second-degree burns
And they hurt but the hurt doesn't matter

The living flame of the world is what matters
The fire is edible, and now

The Fire-Eaters

My home's composed of bricks and dictionaries
A picture of me in a wishing-tree
Five cats
An oven that often doesn't
do what I want it to

My home's composed of bricks and dictionaries
Inflammable, infallible
as you or me

The Day of the Dinosaurs

It was the day when the dinosaurs broke loose
And the salamanders went wild

We closed and opened doors
But it was no use

Lizards like people are allergic to fire
But for some reason the salamander survives

(Prone to fire
Lord of fire)

In fact it figures out the fire
As something which is gold and hot

And which you can emerge from

We closed and opened doors
But it was no use

It was the day when the dinosaurs broke loose
And the salamanders went wild

Poem for a Lady

The lady dances in the crimson mirror of her blood
(Notice that it is not red, but crimson)

She is able to dream of Port Hope and Africa
She is able to be the lady who dances

Huge hats and flowers keep her soul intact
Large bicycles keep her lean and sound

She gets around

Tigers in her mind suggest the colours
Of sun and miraculous sand, but

This lady dances in the crimson mirror of her blood
And peacocks may inform her with their sound

The fact that peacocks also get around
Is not the point, for they have far too many

Colours

This lady moves between bears and tigers
And sometimes peacocks, and sometimes deer

The miracle being that she is both there and here

Know Me

Know me
I have walked through fire for you
I have eaten the apples of wrath and love
I have burned the toes of morning

Know me
I have eaten fire and found it fine
I have walked on the burning coals of God
I have eaten the apples of wrath and love

Know me
Oh Lord of summer I know you know me
Even if I am a profile of night and winter
And walk on coals, and I will come

Copyright © 1976 by Gwendolyn MacEwen

Many of the poems in this book have been broadcast on CBC *Anthology.* "The Carnival" was written for a jazz cantata composed by Ron Collier and first performed by him in Detroit, with Bruno Gerussi as narrator. "Fragments from a Childhood" and "Animal Syllables" first appeared in *Alphabet.* The book was completed with the help of both the Canada Council and the Ontario Arts Council.

ISBN 0 88750 179 6 (hardcover)
ISBN 0 88750 181 8 (softcover)

Printed in Canada

PUBLISHED IN CANADA BY OBERON PRESS